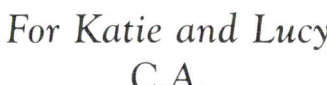

For Katie and Lucy
C.A.

First published 1988 by
Walker Books Ltd
87 Vauxhall Walk
London SE11 5HJ

First printed 1988
Printed and bound by
L.E.G.O., Vicenza, Italy

British Library Cataloguing in Publication Data
West, Colin
I bought my love a tabby cat.
I. Title   II. Anstey, Caroline
821'.914 PZ8.3

ISBN 0-7445-0798-7

I Bought My Love
a Tabby Cat

Written by Colin West
Illustrated by Caroline Anstey

With Best Wishes
love Caroline Anstey 1988.

WALKER BOOKS
LONDON

I bought my love a tabby cat,

A tabby cat, a tabby cat,

My love made him a velvet hat

To wear when we were wed.

I bought my love a billy goat,

A billy goat, a billy goat,

My love made him a woollen coat

To wear when we were wed.

I bought my love a big fat pig,

A big fat pig, a big fat pig,

My love made him a fancy wig

To wear when we were wed.

I bought my love an old grey goose,

 An old grey goose, an old grey goose,

My love made him some dainty shoes

To wear when we were wed.

I bought my love a little mule,

A little mule, a little mule,

My love made him a silken shawl

To wear when we were wed.

I bought my love a talking crow,

A talking crow, a talking crow,

My love made him a handsome bow

To wear when we were wed.

And on the day that we were wed,

That we were wed, that we were wed,

I turned to my true love and said,

"Oh, what a sight to see...

"A tabby cat who wears a hat,

"A billy goat who wears a coat,

"A big fat pig who wears a wig,

"An old grey goose who wears new shoes,

"A little mule who wears a shawl,

"A talking crow who wears a bow,

"Oh, heaven help us, who's to say,

Oh, who's to say, oh, who's to say,

Who is the finest dressed today,

'Tis anyone but me."

But since that day when we were wed,

   When we were wed, when we were wed,

My love makes clothes for me instead,

   As pretty as can be!